Deprived
Expression
Vibes

Jasmine Turner

Deprived Expression Vibes

Charleston, SC
www.PalmettoPublishing.com

Deprived Expression Vibes

Copyright © 2021 by Jasmine Turner

All rights reserved.

No portion of this book may be reproduced, stored in a retrieval system, or transmitted in any form by any means—electronic, mechanical, photocopy, recording, or other—except for brief quotations in printed reviews, without prior permission of the author.

First Edition

Paperback ISBN: 978-1-68515-029-7

My Story—Black in Business

Just a regular girl from the streets of Oakland, California, I came into the world in 1980. Being raised by a single mother, I went through hard times. Working sometimes two or three jobs to keep a roof over our heads and food on the table, my mother struggled, but she always made sure I was taken care of. My father left when I was three years old, so my memories of him when I was a child are foggy. Growing up, I always thought I understood why or knew how it would be to have a father even though he wasn't around, but as I got older, I didn't. The strength and will of having a powerful mother picked up the slack in that area. So I would say I turned out well anyway.

The next phases of my life consisted of some tough growing pains and life lessons to become the person I am today. I was an overachiever, I was told, a go-getter. I set goals for myself after elementary school because I felt I wasn't good enough during those years. Yeah, of course, I was a fun-loving kid who loved music and would sing and play songs to herself. Deep down I was a shy girl with little confidence, a girl who didn't even know her talents could take her somewhere one day. Heck, that little girl didn't know what talents were; she was just doing things for fun.

As a teenager in junior high school, my confidence level got worse. So I challenged myself. I said, "Self, you will be outgoing and participate in activities, and you will make sure that your grade point average is above 3.0 until you graduate from high school." I told myself that every day until I finished high school, and sure enough, I made it through. I graduated with honors. I was a cheerleader and vice president of the student body. I called it my self-check challenge. And every time I felt I was losing myself, I would check it and bring it back down a notch. Oh boy, there were a lot of times when I lost myself, but as a teenager, we all did that, right? LOL! I guess that explains why I need to have control over so many other things in life now.

Trusting people has always been hard for me because there have been so many people who have come into my life who are untrustworthy. Even now and in today's society, trust will take you far with a person like me. Once you show me who you are, I believe you.

After high school came college. I honestly wasn't sure about college at first, but then I thought, *Yeah*, with very high expectations. I was initially accepted into a four-year university, but I decided not to attend. Instead, I attended a local junior college where the tuition was free at that time, and it was conveniently close to home. I could drive every day to school and still get home at a reasonable time to be with family. But even then, a part of me still felt like I was missing out on the bigger experience of it all, and deep down I knew that. College was tough for me. It was the big leagues.

I still managed to keep my self-checks intact. I worked hard in school with hardly any play at all. I mean, some guys liked me here and there, but it was nothing serious. I may have fallen in love a few times but only to get heartbroken in the end. It wasn't okay then, but surely I am over all those heartbreaks because I lived them and learned from every mistake.

Once college ended, I sort of found myself at a crossroads of not knowing what to do next. I had a degree, but I wasn't sure if I wanted to pursue what I went to school for. So I continued to work at my full-time job in banking until I made my decision. Wiped out, I was exhausted even more at the thought of having to go back to school. I had just completed six years of college, and right before that, I was in high school. So I didn't get a chance to have fun the way I wanted to. I was ready to breathe and take a break for a while. However, I did try several times to get into a master's program, but my heart wasn't in it anymore. After being denied time after time, I came back to reality and just said, "I need to work." And at that time the cost of living was getting to be outrageous.

Eventually, I was promoted to personal banker and became one of the top sales representatives in the district. Burned out from all the sales, I decided it was time for me to move on. I decided to pursue something in house or behind the scenes with the same company. Unfortunately, that didn't work so well. Either I didn't have the experience they wanted or most of the departments would only pay me at the same rate if I made a lateral move or I would have to take a pay cut. And I definitely couldn't let that happen.

Continuing to burn out every day from the hustle and bustle of aggressive sales, I realized I would have to start over and acquire new skills that pertained to either being an office assistant/receptionist or an accountant. I had the opportunity to test the waters in both areas to see which one I liked the most.

Needless to say, I had to take a pay cut here and there while going through local temp agencies, but I was okay.

I had some hardship during this time as well. For starters, I was laid off during the recession in 2009. Then a few years later, in 2013, there was a fire in my apartment. I ended up being homeless for about a month until I was able to find a temporary residence until the repairs were done in my apartment. I had to move out, get a storage unit, and live somewhere totally out of my comfort zone. The simple fact that I was even homeless for a while had its challenges. I thought I was losing my mind. I didn't know whether I was coming or going. I can honestly say those were some of the toughest years of my life. It made me see what was important and what was not so important.

I did a lot of growing and soul-searching within myself, and I became wiser. I started to pray a lot and read the Bible and even visited some local churches. It made me stronger, and it didn't kill me. I realized that sometimes you have to walk through fire or be in darkness to come out stronger in the light. It's almost as if you have to find your shine again through the rough growing pains society has to offer. And when society takes a toll on you, it can seem like the whole world is against you.

Once the hardship ended, I was able to move back home to my current address. This time everything was brand new—fresh and clean walls, new carpet, and even new granite countertops. I was so happy because I was finally back home in my comfortable place.

About a year later after moving back home, I finally was able to land a permanent full-time job in a local government agency in the finance department. I was so pleased with myself because one of the biggest dreams that I prayed for came true.

I thought, *I finally got a good job with good benefits and a huge opportunity to learn and grow in the accounting industry.* As soon as I started, I excelled prosperously. How excited I was to be there every day with people who were on the same page as me. Having a job of importance and being able to help people in the community was most important for me. Again, I worked hard, and I challenged myself to learn everything. I wanted to know all about accounting and how it worked and how it flowed. I dug deep into the details of it all in each area of finance and soon realized all the connections in between.

Going back to school to get a master's in accountancy crossed my mind more than a few times, but for some reason, I didn't pursue it. Deep down there was some other force or something else telling me not to go forward in that direction. Looking at different schools and the curriculum of the programs didn't excite me for some reason. So I thought at that point, *Maybe I'm stuck. Maybe I'm living out someone else's dream and I am not fulfilling my true passion.*

Living in the era of COVID-19 has made me realize that accounting is not the only career for me and that my true passion is writing and being able to freely express myself on paper. It excites me and gives me the rush to be creative in my way. Telling stories based on real-life experiences excites me. Writing poems that turn into lyrics and being able to put a rhythm to a rhyme make me smile. Creating a tune of a different vibe and clarifying the sound for the transparency of the ear puts me in a mood to groove, steamrolling my critical-thinking cap into gear and pushing me forward to places I could previously only dream of. I know now that my future is not in accounting; it is definitely in storytelling and music audio production.

With all that being said, I recently started a website blog (http://www.eugenia80.com) with a collection of poetry pieces, video content, music beats produced by me, and the sale of my first poetry book as a first-time published author, *Deprived Expression Vibes*, which I created as a visionary. I came up with a cool concept to create poems based on song titles and albums in my own cool way. From childhood to adulthood, I would take words from conversations that I would have with people and be reminded of a song title or a part of a song lyric and just start belting out the song as a joke or tease to the person I was talking to. I know it's weird, but it was my way of either taking a liking to that person or just me acting silly. So, in the reverse order of that, my poems represent me having a conversation or script, one of my real-life experiences, me just telling a story because my creative mind is flowing, or a mixture of all. For me, that is what will keep my audience curious as to what I will come up with next. It keeps the reader interested and coming back for more. The name *Eugenia80* was created as a dedication to my late grandmother, Eugenia Ogletree. She was always the life of the party and loved playing her music to entertain her company. She was a very outspoken woman with a heart of gold. Her personality endures within me because I have so many memories of her and personality traits that will make you laugh and cry. She held nothing back from living her life. She stood in her truth, and she was never ashamed of that. She was who she was, and if you didn't like it, you could keep moving.

In the essence of that, I came up with three blog website categories. I created "My Playlist Hunt," poetry which is a section intended for DJs and radio personalities to go and find music through the words of my poetry for their sets and playlists. Needless to say, I have noticed that this category has caught on quickly because not only are professional copywriters using my words for music, but they are also using my words for sports, TV, movies, commercials, social media, and the media news. When I finally realized this was happening, I thought, *Wow, I have something good here.*

The last two categories are of concert video content and a music beats playlist because I figured people might as well listen to some tunes while they browse and shop on the website. Overall, this is a fun website, something not to be taken too seriously by the reader at hand. I will advise that most of the content on my website as well as my poetry book and any other content I present should be read by a mature audience. There will be more things to come with this brand and website as it evolves.

All in all, everything that I am doing now is a strong representation of where I started, from that once-shy girl who didn't really speak up at times the way she should have to the girl struggling at times to find her way. The trials and tribulations I have witnessed and been through have brought me to where I am today. I believe that most of my success has come from me learning and excelling in every phase of my life. I am a firm believer in starting from the bottom and working your way up. That is the only way success can drive you to move forward. The point of it all is that if you jump ahead of the game, how will you ever learn or know how to approach an obstacle in the future? This has been my model for years. It is the honest way.

Eugenia80

Table of Vibes

Be a Queen · 1
The First Sight of You · 2
Damn, Is It Safe to Talk? · 3
Trust Your Instincts · 5
Writer's Block Intuition · 6
Spoonings and Cravings · 8
Out the Window · 9
A Taste of My Thoughts · 11
Pen-Game Driven · 12
Sweet Intimate Feelings · 13
In Private We Meet · 14
Indescribable Sensation · 15
Love Bonds · 16
Days Like This… · 17
Lie So Much · 18
Hate and Thieves of 2020 · 19
You Got Me Fucked Up! · 20
Mind over Matter · 21
My Heart · 22
Battered and Bruised · 23
Sad · 24
Done · 25
How You Mental Fight · 26
Looking for My Shot · 28
Stage Presence · 29
Deprived Expression · 30

Be a Queen

Be a queen, don't let these men boss up and throw you off your scheme.
You gotta let them know what you mean.
Tell 'em, "Sit down, shut up, and watch me gleam."
You got this, queen!
Tell 'em, "Take note and don't miss a thing."
I just need you to be there and uplift me when I sing.
Otherwise, you'll be all right. You got a keen insight.
When the enemy is in your space, you take a step back first and observe their stupid face.
I got you now. I can see straight through them, and they don't even know how.
I am a queen. I sit back and watch them watch my scheme.
There's no need to make a scene.
I got you on speed dial if I ever need you for anything.
Love always,
Your queen,

Eugenia80

The First Sight of You

Back by popular demand, with you as I stand. Staying true to the love I have for you.

And although 2020 was a rough year, I found my heart and soul from only one session, it was clear.

One look and I was shook, but I knew then that I would be hooked.

I tried my best to keep my love for you at rest, but I just couldn't help myself.

Those eyes pierced me with one glance and thought, *Hmm… Now there's a face I've never seen in here.*

As he started to stare, his curiosity became more inquisitive with no despair.

I noticed you noticing me, but I didn't realize it at first, you see.

I had to go back and retract my steps, and in very little time, I knew I was on your mind.

It's funny how the eyes have a way of drawing you into a person's soul, but when you played for me, it opened my heart to not be so cold.

I thought, *Are you showing me love in return?* It made me feel like the prettiest girl in the world.

It was at that moment I knew my life would never be the same, but who can you blame?

The attraction was obvious like a hot flame.

And yeah, I hear the stupid chatter, but it will not stop my love for you no matter.

Eugenia80

Damn, Is It Safe to Talk?

Damn, is it safe to talk? Sitting here in a busy parking lot, sipping on green tea matcha; it's hot.
All I can do is think of you and the way that your talents move me.
I just want to be close to you and feel the vibe soothe me.
There is so much uncertainty and fear. The fear of losing you, my dear.
I pray to God every day that you will finally come my way.
We can live out our dreams and make them a reality.
Your spirit grooves me in a way that no other could. Like a man is supposed to treat his lady as he should.
The love you show me is so sincere; I have no doubts and my mind is clear.
2020 changed my whole life and put into gear what has been manifesting inside me for years.
What I have learned up to this point is that transition is never easy. You gotta take your time, go slow, and be the voice of reason.
Oh yeah, but back to me and you, though. I heard we did a duet together recently, fa sho!
Celebrated with joy over listening. The backup sounds of me and you glistening.
I have to say, not bad for my first time on stage. I was nervous, but I wasn't afraid.
I had my protector near to save me if I felt fear. Your music over the years has made me shed some tears.

Only for me to realize that I fell in love with you at a very young age, and that's 100 percent sincere.

That look in your eye captured me then, but it was impossible to dream like that, my friend.

The simple melodies of R&B and the sound of a new generation enlighten me.

Fast-forward two years later, the observation and admiration, the makeover emancipation of a young man and game changer. From then on, I was taken. Not mistaken, never overrated, I'm just elated!

Eugenia8o

Trust Your Instincts

Love always teaches you to love.
It should never teach you to run.
Trust your heart and instincts because what lies ahead is within you, no fuss.
If you keep a mind of your own, it will never leave you alone.
You gotta stand up and be grown.
Show them that you can hold your own because if you are not bold, the world can be cold.
Let the truth be told.
I never thought I'd be told to not push back and just fold.
Your subconscious can be wrong.
Snap out of it and be strong.

Eugenia80

Writer's Block Intuition

I've been sitting around reminiscing for hours, trying to think of what to say. I've worked so long and so hard; with mindless thoughts I've prayed.

Though the one thought that stayed true is the thought of you. And as I listened to you and the others too, I realized that I still love you. ♥

With a love that is so strong and so deep, and as I stand here and write these sheets, my eyes begin to weep.

Scrolling through the feeds of the media, I get a strong premonition, and I know it's my intuition telling me every time to listen.

Suddenly, without a shadow of a doubt, my mind starts to block it out. And I can't see you anymore.

So many thoughts going through my mind right now, like trying to put a rhythm to a rhyme.

Time after time I screw up my mind in the thoughts of you.

But I always come back to "Aww, he's my boo" and that I only want to be with you.

I haven't said anything in a while because I always protect my heart from all the mistakes and fouls.

Day after day I am fighting to keep the anger away in this war on love that people try to take away.

As time moves, I constantly yearn for you and the things you do to become my reality as we connect as two.

For your love, for your touch, for your kiss, I contemplate that I do miss the things I've never said before.

Oh, how I wish you were here right now so we could make love to the moonlight sounds.
Wake up early in your arms' cast of sunshine that keeps me from harm.
Nights that turned into days like this could never keep my spirits in a bad twist.
Next time, if you walk around with a frown, turn it upside down and think about our love and why it all exists.
Just my intuition in bliss.

Eugenia80

Spoonings and Cravings

I felt your touch up against my body as the wind blew and whispered all through the night.

Those big strong hands holding me tight as the moon stayed, stealing soft kisses from Mr. Good Night.

As the kissing goes longer, our bodies start to rumble, and the feelings got me stumbled.

"Oh my goodness, this feels so good," as my mind starts to wander.

The things I want to do with you have got me with a love that's so true. I hope I see you soon because my cravings are only for my boo.

Manifestation like this leaves my body in a twist while the brain stays healthy with a mindset you just can't resist.

My love for you runs deep, and I have fallen to complete.

Like downs on a play, I take it day by day and pray that you'll come to me someday.

Oh, how I love thee, let me count the ways. You are my safe place, and that's all I can say. ♥♥♥

Eugenia80

Out the Window

As I look out the window into the sky, the rain falls like shiny diamonds on the rise.

I think to myself, *Babe, is that you?* I feel your presence all around me when I am blue.

Oh, how I miss you. And I can't wait to meet you. I just don't know what to do.

But as I told you before, I am following my heart instead of running like a scared sour gummy tart.

I can picture it now, that first official glance, and nothing will stop us, how?

They say we shouldn't be together, but I feel in my heart that this love will last forever.

You make me feel brand new, like a warm, fluffy biscuit with jam soft to chew. I just love you.

You check all my boxes and some. You keep me on my toes when they are numb.

Even though sometimes I want to run, I end up running right back into your arms, where it has begun.

And though it hurts at times, my faith in God is what's keeping this love we have alive.

I love you so much, and I can't wait to feel your touch.

Those big strong hands all over my body; you are the man.

The one whom I have been waiting for my whole life. You complete my soul day and night.

You feed my spirit on a deeper level, a level that no one else understands, not even an average fellow on a hot day with a fan.

Only me, you, and God go hand and hand, like sunflowers bright and yellow planted in a can.

Eugenia80

A Taste of My Thoughts

Meditate and be great.
Open your mind, like fine wine.
Go ahead and take a sip, let it dip.
I got the remedy if you think you can handle this shit.
Do not waste time being blind.
Open your eyes and see it's time.
Moving on to celebrate what I have accomplished to date.
So do not hate, find your escape and the blessing that the Lord has on your plate.
Do not throw it away, let it marinate, cook; have a feast and do not delay.
Wash it down with a beverage, sleep well with no disparage.
Enjoy your pleasures and keep getting better.
This is a taste of my thoughts!

Eugenia80

Pen-Game Driven

Thinking of you makes me feel blue.
All I wanted was a chance to be with you.
Now I don't even know what's true.
You got me open and not having a clue.
I really do love you.
No lies, no cap, I know I'm not the average cat.
But you have put me in a position that has muthafuckas wishing they can sit here and spit like that.
I'm telling you, you had me at first look and the pen game is so off the hook.
I told you that a time or two.
It inspired me to pursue.
A love so deep in my heart that I can feel the beat in my heart.
My soul is taking me now to places that have awakened me, and I don't know how.
My spirit has risen, and I write every time I am driven.
It keeps all my thoughts clear and keeps me sincere.
All the bullshit out, without casting a doubt.
I take pride in myself because self-care can be your wealth.

Eugenia80

Sweet Intimate Feelings

I can't wait for the day to be in your arms. You make me feel brand new and want to reach for the stars.
Your love is like sunshine even on a cloudy day. My feelings for you are real like the moonlight with sex appeal.
As the moon shines bright, the love scene comes to light.
Your love is warm, like a cozy fire in a midnight storm.
Your love is so kind, my eyes stay focused on you; I'm not blind.
Your love is so simple like those sexy dimples.
You make me laugh when I am blue. You bring me joy when I see you.
The thought of you has no filter in my mind, and when I think of you, my love is humble and kind.
Sweet like an apple pie with cinnamon on my mind.
Sugar on a stick that melts in your mouth when you bite into it with one lick.
Mmm…now that's a kick.

Eugenia80

In Private We Meet

Waiting for us to meet so that I am not nervous when we speak.
You've given me butterflies for weeks because your love is just so damn unique.
I want to feel your skin from within and take it slow on a weekend.
It's important that in private we meet because its nobody else's business what the conversation will be.
You had me at hello, no doubt, but when you sang to me, it made me want to shout.
Shout your name in bed, under the stars, or in the rain instead.
Where the moonlight appears in your arms, I am never afraid with all your charm.
I love you even when you are not near, and I know you're happy when you are drinking a beer.
You gave me hope last year.
When all your admiration and dedication set into gear.
I will never forget that for as long as I live.
You made my year!!! :)
Put a smile on my face, *Cheers!*

Eugenia80

Indescribable Sensation

Words can't describe anymore how I feel inside.
All I know is that I yearn for you.
With a constant burn in my soul that doesn't want to shake us because we're not through.
I was sitting back the other day reading up on my self-fulfilling prophecy, thinking, *Is this true?*
And then I thought, *Yes, because the vibe always puts me in the mood.*
Dreams of kissing you as I meditate give me tingles in the pit of my stomach.
The thought of us touching skin to skin, lying in bed for days as we get it in.
Making love as the sun comes up slowly, you whisper in my ear, "You are my one and only."
I love you so much I just can't leave you alone.
You are my best friend, my confidant, my sole purpose here.
I am so blessed and happy that you are my listening ear.
You understand my pains; you understand my struggles.
You lift me when I am in trouble.
This brings me back to the prophecy; it's true.
I know now for sure that I want to marry you too.
I love you!

Eugenia80

Love Bonds

When I think of our love, it fits like a glove. Glue from a tube that's stuck on you.

A deeper love that all would argue, but only you and I know the truth, it's not a bargain.

Our love is just a reminder that we have a bond, a bond so unbreakable that it can be described in the form of chemical bonds.

Do you know much about chemistry?

Well, that's how I would describe this feeling.

You see, a covalent bond is the strongest bond to be created in chemistry.

Like two strong magnets at collision, it's snappy.

For example,

If you take us and face us back to each other, wrap a thick band around as the band starts to resist us,

We start to walk away, but our bodies start to miss us.

As we try to walk away and the more and more we try, the band will snap and pull us back together, no lie.

The toughest resistance in chemistry describes our bond, and we just can't resist being apart from each other; this love will never die.

Our chemistry is strong.

Our chemistry is solid.

We love each other more and more each day for our support and knowledge.

Eugenia8o

Days Like This...

It's days like this that always have a fucking plot twist. I wish I knew what the fuck was going on, but I will keep on moving forward strong.
"Keep calm," they say to me.
I say, "I am calm. What the fuck else do you want from me?"
I say to that, keep it real, assholes.
They say nothing, not even a mumble or an utter.
It's days like this that I ask you, "Do you trust me?" I wonder.
It's all a mystery, none other.
How dare you judge me? What nerve. Next time look in the mirror and stop being a perve.
I'm sick and tired of your bullshit. I'm sick and tired of how you play games and get a kick.
I really did love you and maybe I still do, but with all the games and sabotage I don't even know if this is true.
So I pose a question to you: Do you really know how to love a woman like you say you do, or is it all an act for the cast and crew?
Hmm???

Eugenia80

Lie So Much

Why do people lie so much? It's enough to make you cry so much.

A lie is a lie. It's not a slice of apple pie.

So next time you decide to lie, think about who it will affect and who it will deny.

You can cause a lot of damage when you lie. Just keep my name out of your mouth next time.

So much has been said since then, but we can't go back and undo the damage again.

People just need to understand that lies are created to destroy you, not to lift you and uphold you.

Lies are not meant to be fruitful. They create a habit that repeats and is unuseful.

So don't stir the pot because the spoon might be too hot. *Ouch!*

I could never trust a liar. The aura and energy sets me on fire.

God said, "The truth will set you free." And I stand by that 100 percent—that's key.

So think before you speak, and you'll be amazed at what comes to mind and not up a creek.

Because paddling up that creek can get lonely, and it can lead to desperation and phony.

Soon you'll be drowning in lies with no way out, looking for help with no one to shout.

Be consistent, tell the truth, stop the lies, and be a troop.

Don't be a goof because I am not impressed by you.

Eugenia80

Hate and Thieves of 2020

You hate on my money because you think it's funny.
You hate on my site because of whom I like.
Stay out of my business, stand by, and continue to witness the great expression and my divine blessing.
Never knew what I had until I actually got sad.
I dug down deep and solidified the strength in me.
Don't poke the bear while she is asleep because you never know what you'll get while you creep.
The lion in me is always hunting.
Always observing, always listening, and never fronting.
I stay focused with my eyes on the prize.
Some may try to distract me, but I never compromise.
I mean what I say and say what I mean.
Don't ever come for me if you think I'll just leave.
You stole from me, and I want my money.
That's the least you can do for all the promotion and honey.

Eugenia80

You Got Me Fucked Up!

You coming at me with all this dirt, and you go behind my back with insults and a curse.
He who laughs last laughs first. Next time look in the mirror and don't choke.
'Cause when you bark up this tree, I go cold.
Looking forward to big dreams never gets old.
Yeah, I got a bone to pick now, and you know.
Haters are watching my moves up close.
Yeah, I know you like what you see, asshole.
When you fuck with a lady, you better turn, but when you fuck with a boss, you get served.
Listen, I come in peace and love. I always play fair, not afraid to speak up when you dare.
You got a problem with how I do my thing? I suggest you step down and watch me sing.
'Cause when the ching starts to roll, I'm going to bling.
I'll continue my craft 'cause it's my new hobby for now.
Better yet, I think I'll sit back relax and enjoy the crowd.
Punk ass bitches!!!
I said, "Keep it real from the jump," and you all clowned.
You got me fucked up all day 'cause I mean what I say: ain't no need in sticking around, okay.
Peace!!!

Eugenia80

Mind over Matter

Be bold, be strong, never let anyone steer you wrong.

Have courage, have faith. Open your eyes and see through the lying snakes.

Because those faces will appear when your game is up and your pride is not interfered.

They'll try to drag you down and make you believe that something is fatigued.

But you must stay up and intrigue your mind and where it will lead.

Be a leader, not a follower, my mom always told me.

I live my life the way I want to; however, some try to impede.

Some may call it boring; some may say I'm lonely.

But I call it not living for the phony.

So don't get down on yourself.

Go back out there, keep trying, and reach out if you need help.

When expectations are high, you must remember: a positive mind over matter always wins the fight and flies.

Eugenia80

My Heart

I have a heart, and it's red.
But it can change to other colors if it's taken for granted or spared.
Don't break my heart, please, I say to you.
All these foolish games are really tiring, and I am through.
You made me feel special at one point, uplifted and hard to lose.
The kind of love that made your fellas stop and stare because they were jealous.
The envy had them embarrassed, so much so they couldn't stand us.
Trying to reciprocate what we have.
You got to try a little harder than that, fellas, in order to make it last.
To my one true love, back to me and you, my heart is still red for the only one who has a clue.

Eugenia80

Battered and Bruised

Battered and bruised in silence by the scars she infused.
A woman with no direction and nowhere to go has everything to lose.
If you take the woman out of silence even for just a little while,
There is happiness that appears and the showing of true love that shuts those fears.
I met a man once who promised to love me dear,
But even after giving all my love away, he didn't even care, nor did he shed a tear.
I don't really know the full truth as to why his love changed.
All I know is that he came home one day and started to slap me in the face.
I speculated that drugs were the case, and soon it came to be that he was barely standing and wobbling all over the place.
He started lying to me and coming home real late.
Purse full of money, fresh off payday.
Fall asleep overnight and wake up in the morning, and I was thinking, *No way.*
All my money stolen, gone with bills due to pay.
The abuse continued until I was fed up,
Sneaking to pack my things within dirty laundry he snubbed.
Finally, the runaway day come to set me free.
Off in a secret hiding place awaited my big dream.
Most women aren't so lucky, you see.
You have to be strong-willed and have a soul that wants peace.

Eugenia80

Sad

This is dedicated to the sad one.

Don't be sad; you should be glad. That you had a burden taken off your ass.

I'm not sad; hell, I'm not even mad because the decision was to make an honest bag.

I walk by faith, not by sight: God told me to let that pain take a hike.

So now I am free with the weight lifted off me. I am ready to see where life takes me.

It took me a while to realize just how special my thoughts are of a prize.

And now you know how it feels to have your heart taken on a thrill.

Once upon a time, my love for you was deep, and you used me like a cheap piece of meat.

Go to hell, asshole, 'cause see, now I know my meat is worthy and all my curves are smooth and swerved.

I hope you enjoyed it while it lasted because now my confidence has taken off and blasted.

The universe is guiding me on a spiritual enlightening.

And the sun is always shining on me, as my moon man looks after me.

So don't be sad, the past is in the past. As I write this in the present, my future is embedded with so much love, abundance, and joy that has been granted.

Eugenia80

Done

When you done, you done.
Bye-bye for now, gotta run.
But before I go, let me touch you with these quotes.
I left my keys at the door.
I finalized some bills so that way you wouldn't wonder still.
I shut down the computer as a final farewell to you.
I left everything in its place, but I took my stuffed animals because they can't be replaced.
As I clean up this space, my first thought is, *Will I miss this place?*
Oh yeah, *hell naw*, that's right. I have a new future to embrace.
You see, you made that possible for me in 2020.
My plans go as far as thy I can see.
Thanks again for the opportunity.
It's been a real pleasure, and it's nothing new to me.
Moving toward goals set, I keep moving forward.
I'm done!

Eugenia80

How You Mental Fight

I stay calm
I play fair
I write rhymes, and I don't commit crimes.
You gotta grind
You gotta climb
You gotta shine and leave nothing behind.
If you bend
If you spin
When you win, represent, and don't let it end.
They see you moving
They see you grooving
They see you cruising, but they won't stop until they see you losing.
The devil is real
The devil is ill
The devil will steal if you let him, he will destroy and kill.
Stay on your game
Stay on your claim
Stay on your aim, don't be the one that they blame.
Be the light
Be the flight
Be the hype, don't slow down that winning fight.
What a thrill
What a deal
What a spill, don't stop now to chill.
Keep going
Keep showing

Deprived Expression Vibes

Keep flowing, you got this, you already knowing.
Bring the pain
Bring the shame
Bring the flame, zap 1, zap 2, keep them entertained.
Find the shot
Find the spot
Find the hop, get the roll, and pop.
Hocus
Pocus
Solstice, stand behind the screen so you can focus.
Energy
Synergy
Mentoring, inspiration is so groundbreaking and centering.

Eugenia80

Looking for My Shot

In lab all day, I ain't got no time to play.
When I sit and parlay, I find that I have a lot to say.
Life's been crazy since 2020 led the way.
A lot of shit's been happening with all the COVID-19 stuff, okay.
I'd like my shot, please, sir, so I can continue on my way.
I often wonder where I'd be if life was the same for me.
I finally pulled it together and sought out my big dream.
I love writing now, such artistry and so free.
Expression in this form is key when you can't internalize your speech.

Eugenia80

Stage Presence

Lights flashing, camera, action.
The sound is bumping and always maxing.
The crowds swaying from side to side as your sing and play style has got them going wild.
As you sparked, up the charts, we still remember how you made your mark.
You looked good as you stood on that stage giving it up to the hood.
So pleased with all ease, so smooth and sweet. You've got this thing that makes us all want to sing.
Vocals were strong and never wrong. Chords right with a track that never bites.
All blue, that's all you.
Shades dark, blowing kisses from the heart.
It's that swag, baby, it never lags.
So real, you are the deal. I jumped out of my seat just to get a close-up for the thrill.
Stage presence, a gracious and sexy essence.

Eugenia80

Deprived Expression

Admiring my creative side.
Please don't get offended by these rhymes.
I promise you I'm not a hoe.
I was just exposed by several creeps who wouldn't go and leave me alone.
But now that I have your attention, I have to mention that my true identity is sentimental.
Clear as a pixel, like fine fancy crystals.
We all have a freaky side, you can't deny.
I just choose to express this side because it's been deprived.
Next time don't judge, you little scrub.
There's only one judge I answer to, and that's the man above.
And yeah, I know my man is good, he's understood.
Maybe you should have treated him better.
I never would.
Moving on from petty games, you should be ashamed.
The blame is on you now; I can't complain.
Because even despite, my future still looks bright.
I got a lot on my plate now, and I know you wanna bite.

Eugenia80

Acknowledgements

I'd like to begin by thanking God, my Lord and savior. Without him I wouldn't have made it through any of the storms that I faced head-on in my life. Secondly, I'd like to thank my mother, Evelyn Austin Turner, for raising a very bright, intelligent, and sweet young lady into womanhood. You and I have been through many hardships together, and we've survived them all standing tall. Thank you for teaching me how to be strong. I would also like to thank my dad, David Turner. We weren't that close when I was a child; however, as I grew older, I realized the importance of having you around. Thank you for teaching me how to forgive. To the rest of my family and friends, thank you for the continued love and support as I go through this journey called life. And thank you to everyone else (my readers) for all your support as well. Lastly, I'd like to thank myself for the mental fight of reprioritizing my focus and coming into my own with a hobby that once was hidden and is now my revelation.

Author: Jasmine Turner
Business: Eugenia8o
https://www.eugenia8o.com

www.ingramcontent.com/pod-product-compliance
Lightning Source LLC
LaVergne TN
LVHW011900060526
838200LV00054B/4451